ROXABOXEN

ALICE McLERRAN
ROXABOXEN

ILLUSTRATED BY
BARBARA COONEY

Lothrop, Lee & Shepard Books
New York

This edition is published by special arrangement with Lothrop, Lee
& Shepard Books, a division of William Morrow & Company, Inc.

Grateful acknowledgment is made to Lothrop, Lee & Shepard Books, a
division of William Morrow & Company, Inc. for permission to reprint
Roxaboxen by Alice McLerran, illustrated by Barbara Cooney. Text
copyright © 1991 by Alice McLerran; illustrations copyright © 1991 by
Barbara Cooney.

Printed in the United States of America

ISBN 0-15-302173-X

4 5 6 7 8 9 10   035   97 96 95

To May Cargill Doan and all her line   —A.M.

For my Roxaboxen guide, Tahe   —B.C.

Marian called it Roxaboxen.
(She always knew the name of everything.)
There across the road, it looked like any rocky hill—
nothing but sand and rocks, some old wooden boxes,
cactus and greasewood and thorny ocotillo—
but it was a special place.

The street between Roxaboxen and the houses curved like a river,
so Marian named it the River Rhode.
After that you had to ford a river to reach Roxaboxen.

Of course all of Marian's sisters came:
Anna May and Frances and little Jean.
Charles from next door, even though he was twelve.
Oh, and Eleanor, naturally,
and Jamie with his brother Paul.
Later on there were others, but these were the first.

Well, not really the first.
Roxaboxen had always been there
and must have belonged to others, long before.

When Marian dug up a tin box filled with round black pebbles
everyone knew what it was:
it was a buried treasure.
Those pebbles were the money of Roxaboxen.
You could still find others like them if you looked hard enough.
So some days became treasure-hunting days, with everybody trying to
    find that special kind.
And then on other days you might just find one without even looking.

A town of Roxaboxen began to grow, traced in lines of stone:
Main Street first, edged with the whitest ones,
and then the houses.
Charles made his of the biggest stones.
After all, he was the oldest.
At first the houses were very plain, but soon they all began to
  add more rooms.
The old wooden boxes could be shelves or tables or anything you wanted.
You could find pieces of pottery for dishes.
Round pieces were best.

Later on there was a town hall.
Marian was mayor, of course;
that was just the way she was.
Nobody minded.

After a while they added other streets.
Frances moved to one of them and built herself a new house outlined
   in desert glass,
bits of amber, amethyst, and sea-green:
a house of jewels.

And because everybody had plenty of money,
there were plenty of shops.
Jean helped Anna May in the bakery—
pies and cakes and bread baked warm in the sun.
There were two ice cream parlors.
Was Paul's ice cream the best, or Eleanor's?
Everybody kept trying them both.
(In Roxaboxen you can eat all the ice cream you want.)

Everybody had a car.
All you needed was something round for a
   steering wheel.
Of course, if you broke the speed limit you had to go to jail.
The jail had cactus on the floor to make it uncomfortable,
and Jamie was the policeman.
Anna May, quiet little Anna May, was always speeding—
you'd think she liked to go to jail.

But ah, if you had a horse, you could go as fast as the wind.
There were no speed limits for horses,
and you didn't have to stay on the roads.

All you needed for a horse was a stick and some kind of bridle,
and you could gallop anywhere.

Sometimes there were wars.

Once there was a great war, boys against girls.

Charles and Marian were the generals.

The girls had Fort Irene, and they were all girl scouts.

The boys made a fort at the other end of Roxaboxen, and they were
    all bandits.

All you needed for a horse was a stick and some kind of bridle,
and you could gallop anywhere.

Sometimes there were wars.

Once there was a great war, boys against girls.

Charles and Marian were the generals.

The girls had Fort Irene, and they were all girl scouts.

The boys made a fort at the other end of Roxaboxen, and they were
all bandits.

Oh, the raids were fierce, loud with whooping and the stamping
   of horses!
The whirling swords of ocotillo had sharp thorns—
but when you reached your fort you were safe.

Roxaboxen had a cemetery, in case anyone died,
but the only grave in it was for a dead lizard.
Each year when the cactus bloomed, they decorated the grave
    with flowers.

Sometimes in the winter, when everybody was at school and the
   weather was bad,
no one went to Roxaboxen at all, not for weeks and weeks.
But it didn't matter;
Roxaboxen was always waiting.
Roxaboxen was always there.
And spring came, and the ocotillo blossomed,
and everybody sucked the honey from its flowers,
and everybody built new rooms, and everybody decided to have
   jeweled windows.
That summer there were three new houses on the east slope
and two new shops on Main Street.

And so it went.
The seasons changed, and the years went by.
Roxaboxen was always there.

The years went by, and the seasons changed,
until at last the friends had all grown tall,
and one by one, they moved away
to other houses, to other towns.
So you might think that was the end of Roxaboxen—
but oh, no.

Because none of them ever forgot Roxaboxen.
Not one of them ever forgot.
Years later, Marian's children listened to stories of that place
and fell asleep dreaming dreams of Roxaboxen.
Gray-haired Charles picked up a black pebble on the beach
   and stood holding it,
remembering Roxaboxen.

More than fifty years later, Frances went back
and Roxaboxen was still there.
She could see the white stones bordering Main Street,
and there where she had built her house
the desert glass still glowed—
amethyst, amber, and sea-green.

On a hill on the southeast corner of Second Avenue and Eighth Street, in Yuma, Arizona, there is a place once known as Roxaboxen. The events in this book really happened—to Alice McLerran's mother.

With the aid of her mother's childhood manuscript, the memories of relatives, and letters and maps from the former inhabitants of Roxaboxen, Alice McLerran was able to recreate that magical world as if she had played there herself. She presents us with "a celebration of the active imagination, of the ability of children to create, even with the most unpromising materials, a world of fantasy so real and multidimensional that it earns a lasting place in memory."

Artist Barbara Cooney saw Roxaboxen as one of her "toughest assignments yet: constructing a magical world out of something that wasn't there." She made two trips to the desert, where she found "a small tan hill dotted with stones and rocks, a scattering of desert plants, and now lots of broken glass and an old car chassis." But accompanied by Alice McLerran's eighty-year-old Aunt Frances (former Roxaboxenite), the magic and spirit of Roxaboxen began to emerge—a magic found in the minds and hearts of the children who played there.